HOW T DRAW

FOR KIDS AGES 4-8

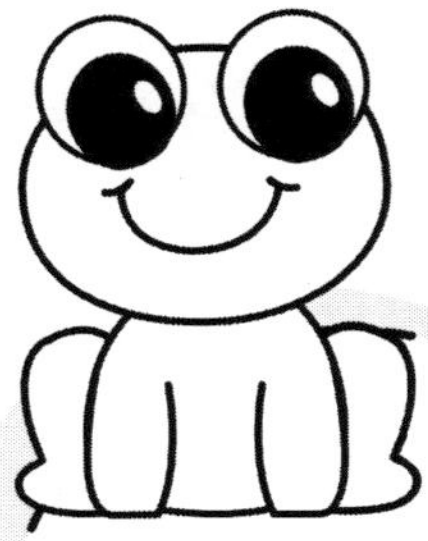

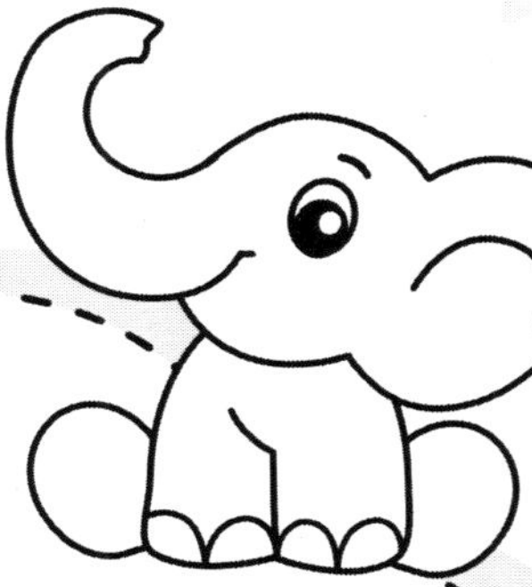

This book belongs to:

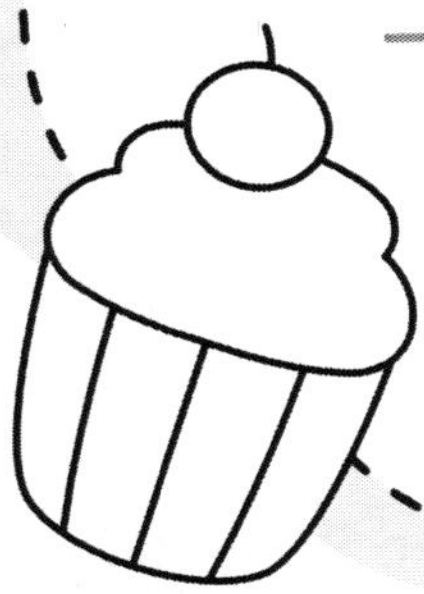

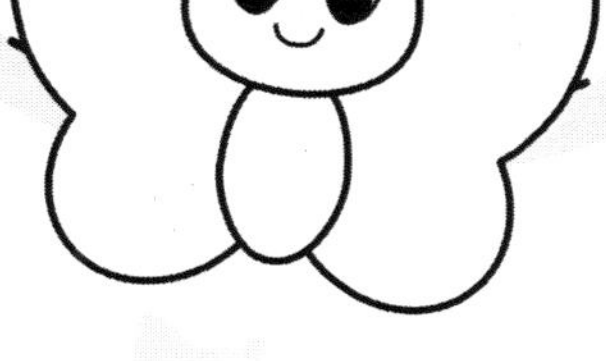

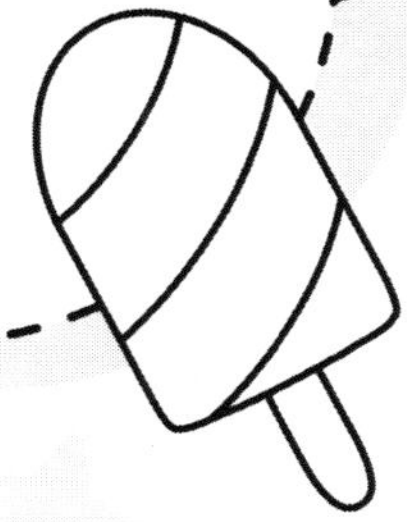

_____

Created by

☆ Thank you for your purchase ☆

We hope this book helps your kids improve their motor skills, discover new hobbies, boost self-confidence, find a healthy way to release emotion and so much more!

Contact us: www.rvappstudios.com

Copyright © 2023 Lucas & Friends by RV AppStudios

All rights reserved.

No portion of the book may be duplicated, saved in a database, or transmitted using any technology without the publisher's prior written consent or as specifically authorized by law, a license, or terms negotiated with the relevant body that manages reproduction rights (U.S. Copyright Law).

First paperback edition **May 2023**

Designed by: RV AppStudios Team

ISBN: 9781960790217

About us

We create amazing children educational books for babies, toddlers, and little kids. Lucas & Friends by RV AppStudios is one of largest children's mobile app developers in the world. Over 150 million kids will play with our apps this year, and that's for free and with no ads.

Learn to draw

Let's draw a beautiful eye
A step-by-step guide

1

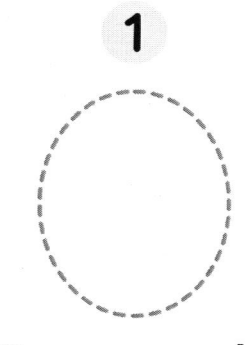

Draw an oval.

2

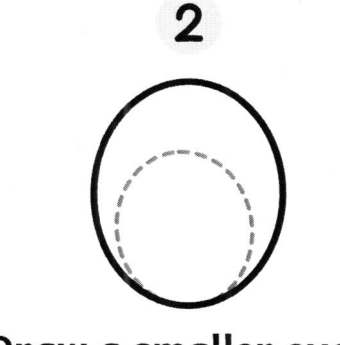

Draw a smaller oval.

3

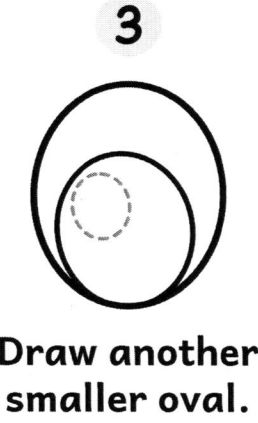

Draw another smaller oval.

4

Color the second oval black.

5

Great job, you've drawn a beautiful eye!

House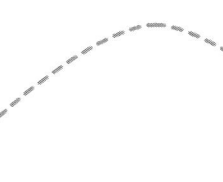

1

2

3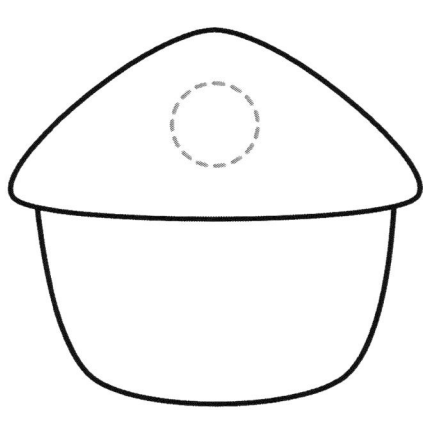

4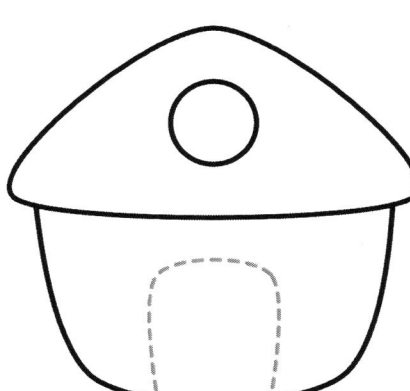

5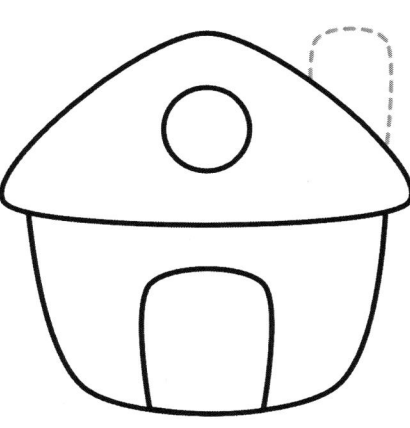

Trace

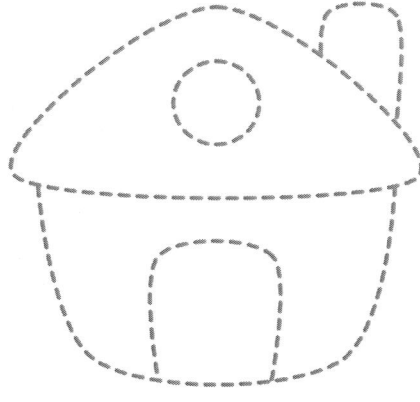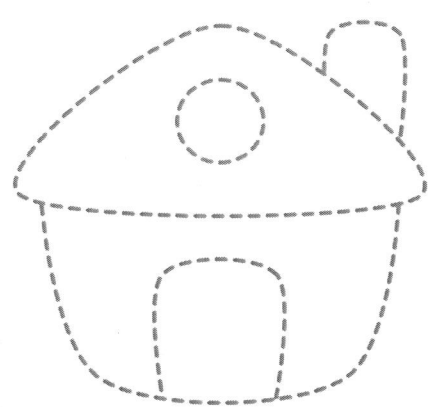

Draw

Butterfly

1
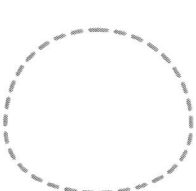

2

3

4

5

6

Trace

Draw

Duck

1

3

5

Trace

Draw

Cake

1

2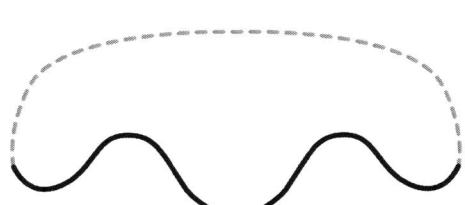

3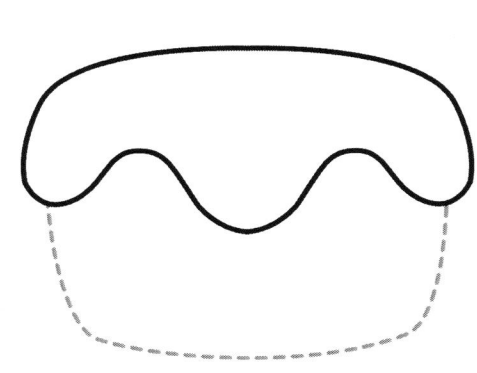

4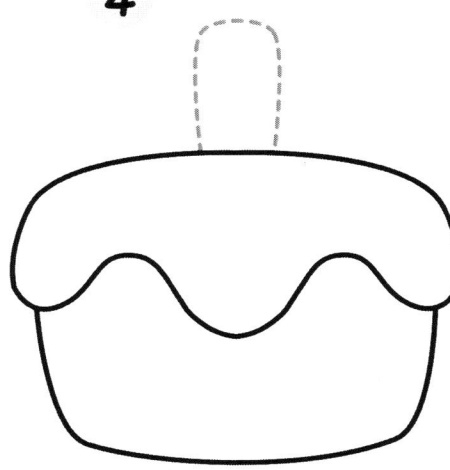

5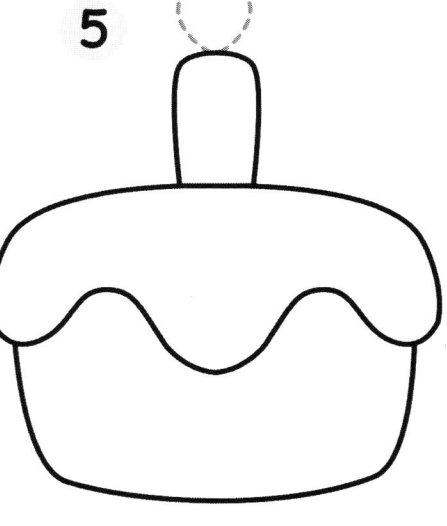

Trace

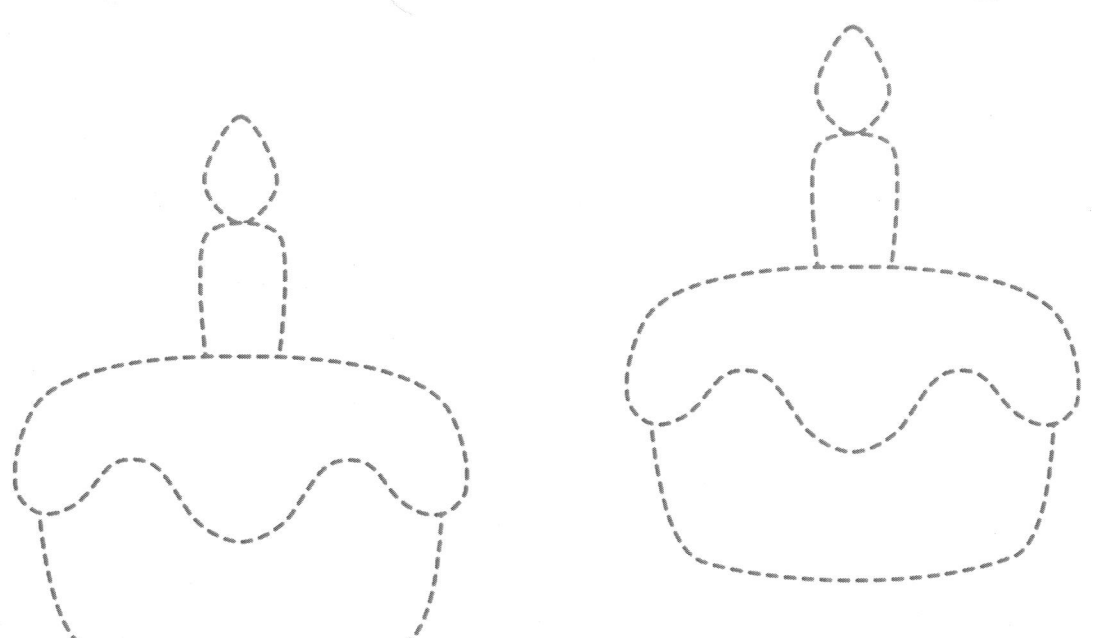

Draw

Ship

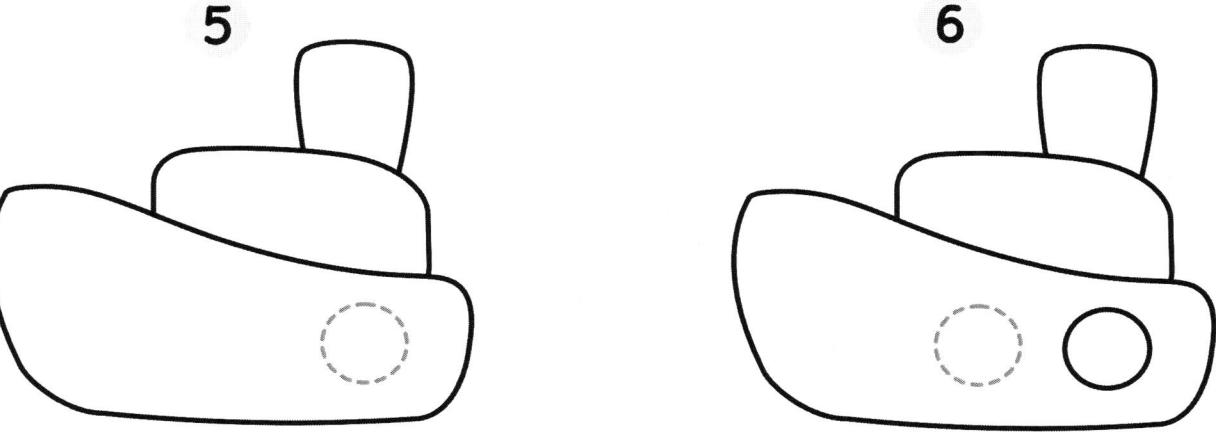

Trace

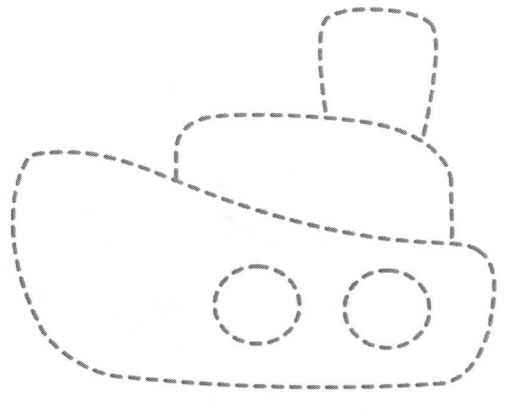
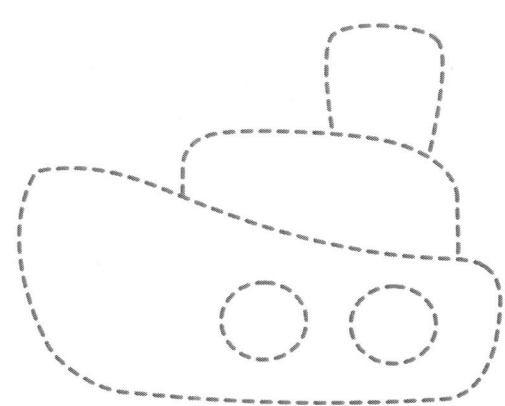

Draw

Fish

1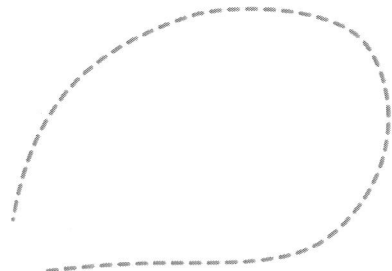

2

3

4

Trace

Draw

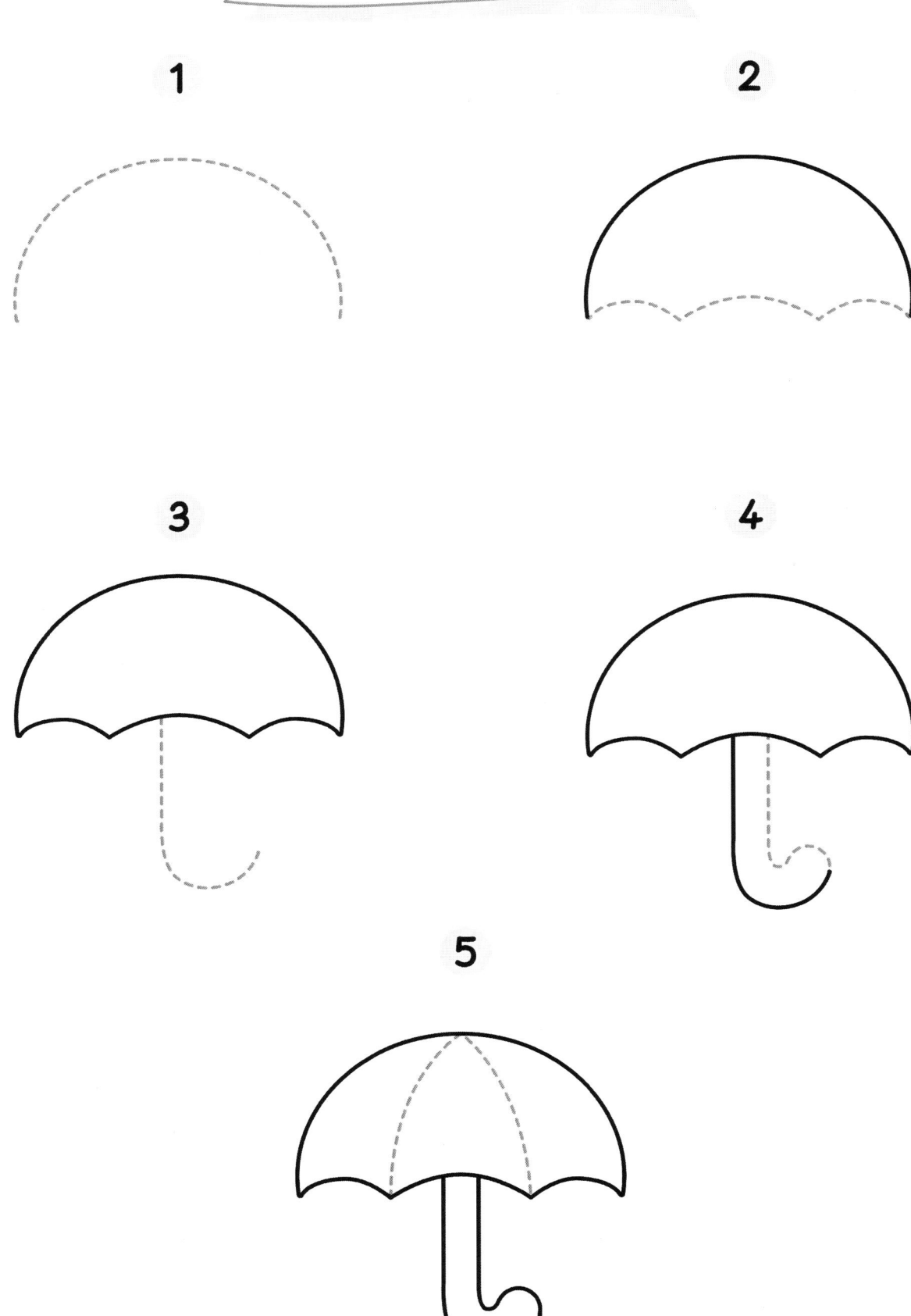

Trace

Draw

Ladybug

1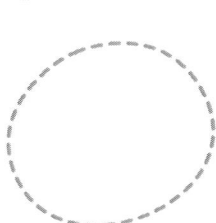

2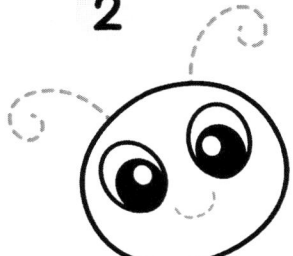

3

4

5

6

Trace

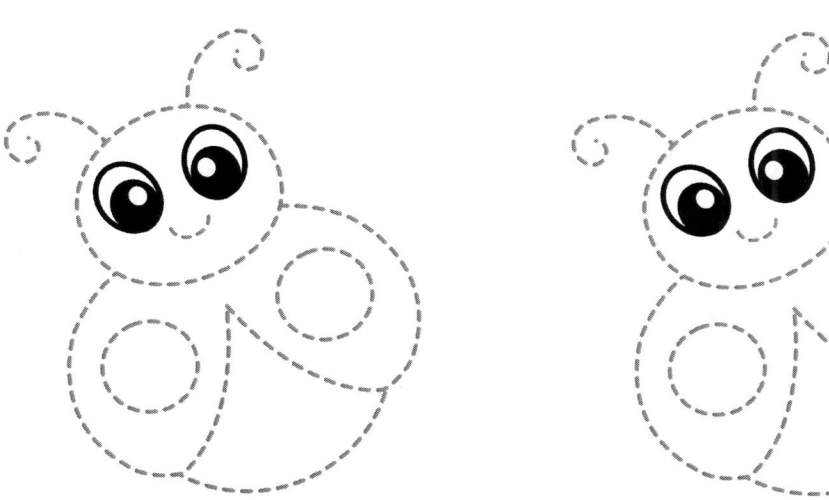

Draw

Candy

1

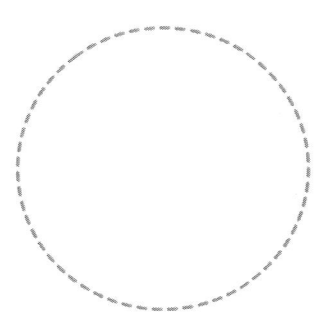

2

3

4

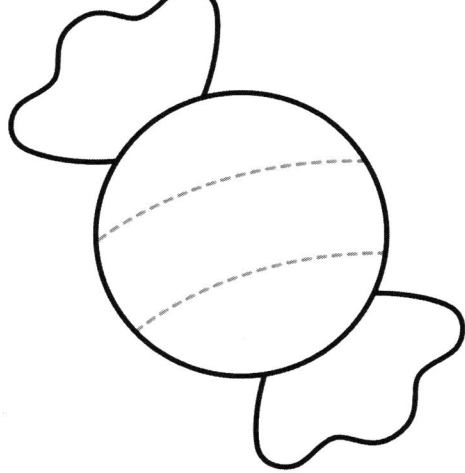

Trace

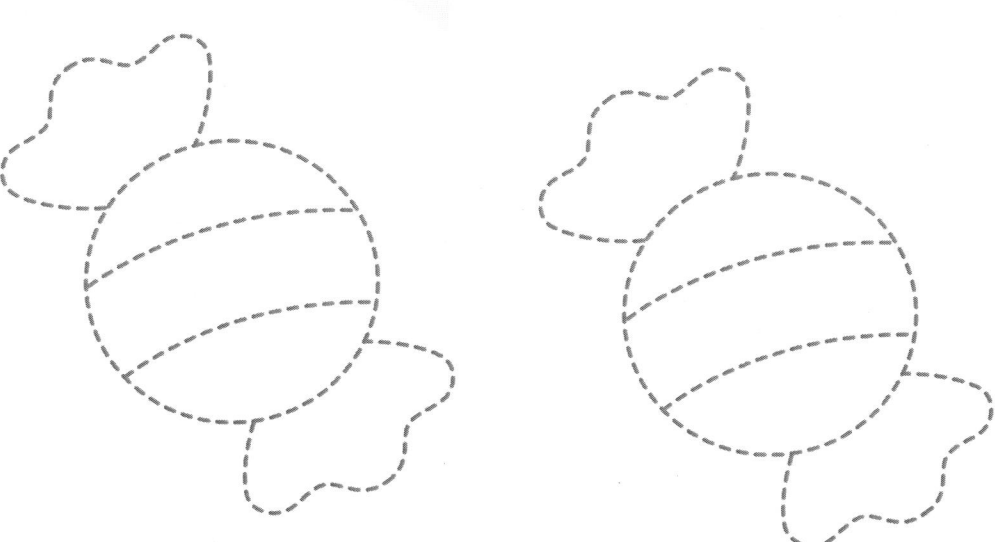

Draw

Crown

1
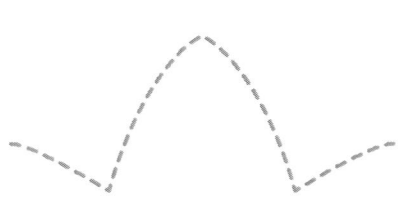

2
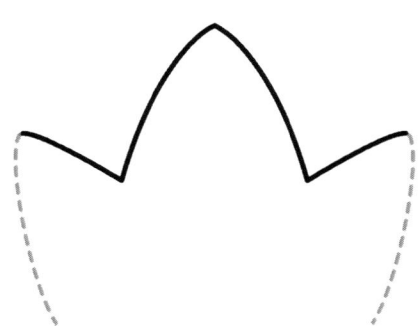

3
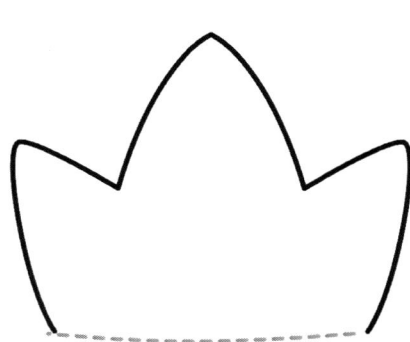

4

5

Trace

Draw

Snail

1

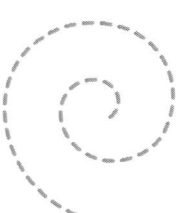

2

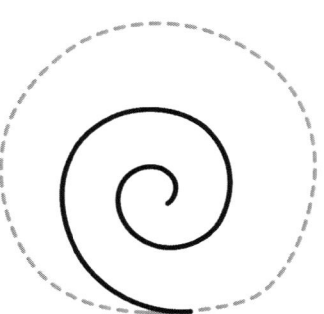

3

4

5

Trace

Draw

Moon

1

2

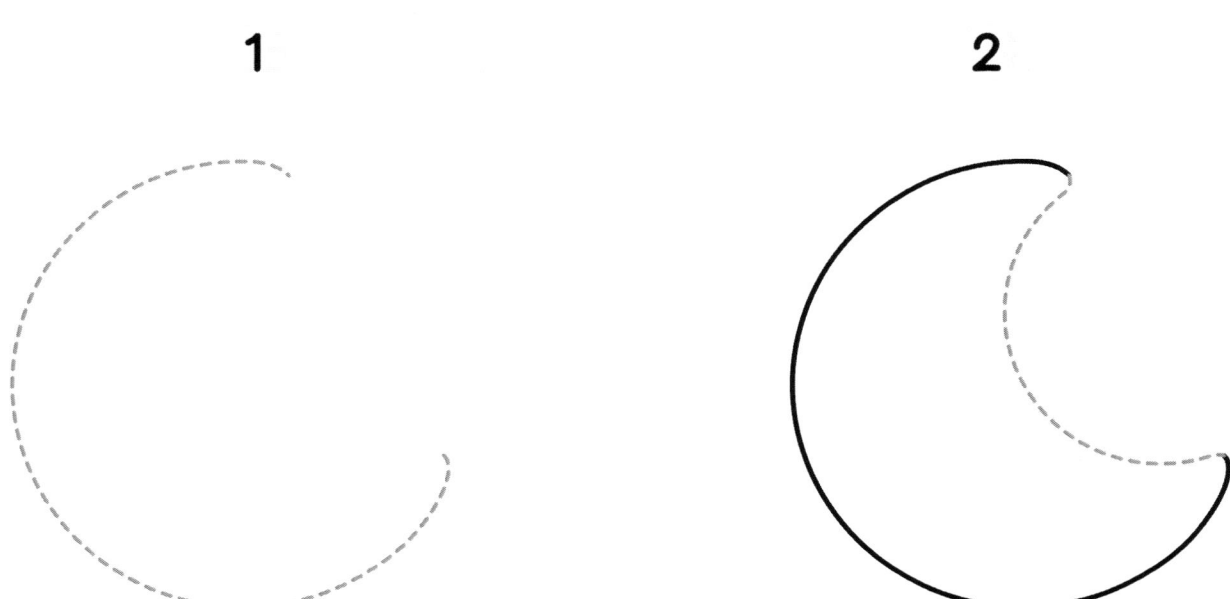

3

Trace

Draw

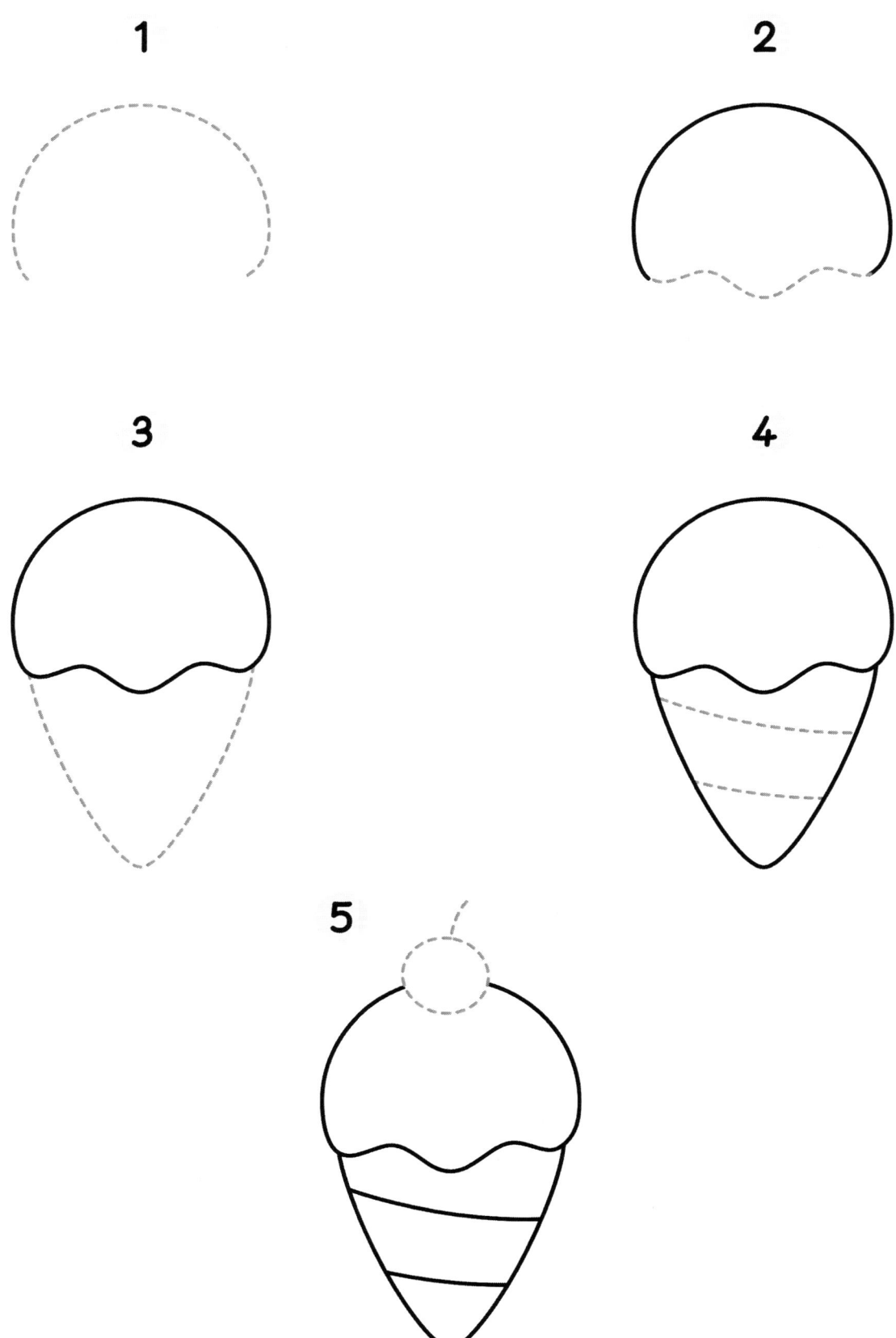

Trace

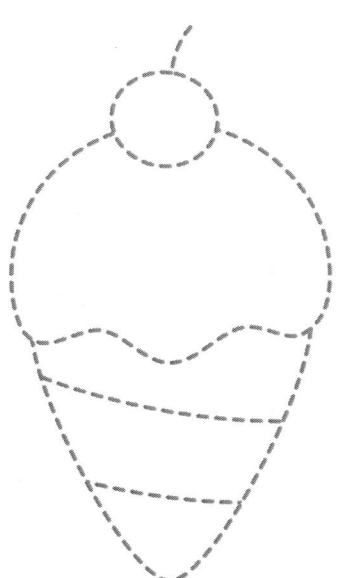 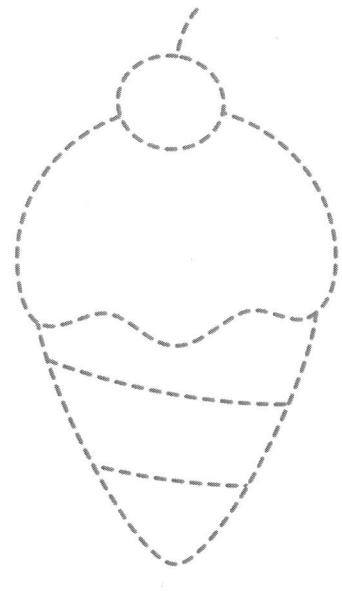

Draw

Caterpillar

1
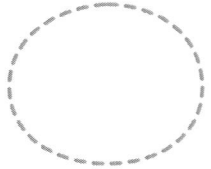

2

3

4

5

6

Trace

Draw

Christmas tree

1

2

3

4

5

6

Trace

Draw

Teddy

1
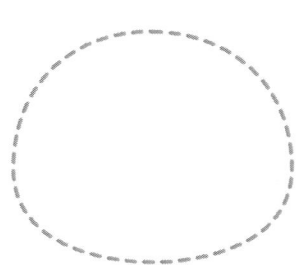

2

3

4

5

6

Trace

Draw

Drum

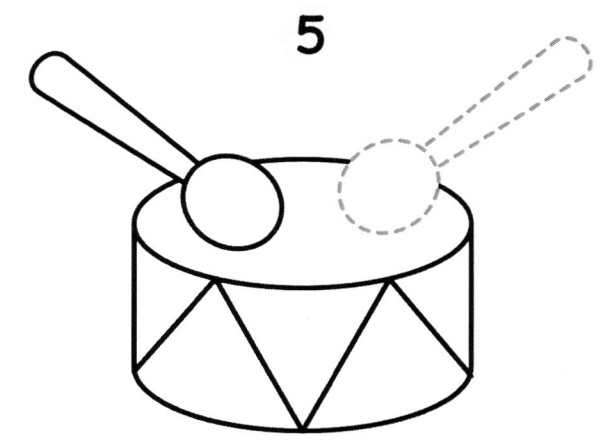

Trace

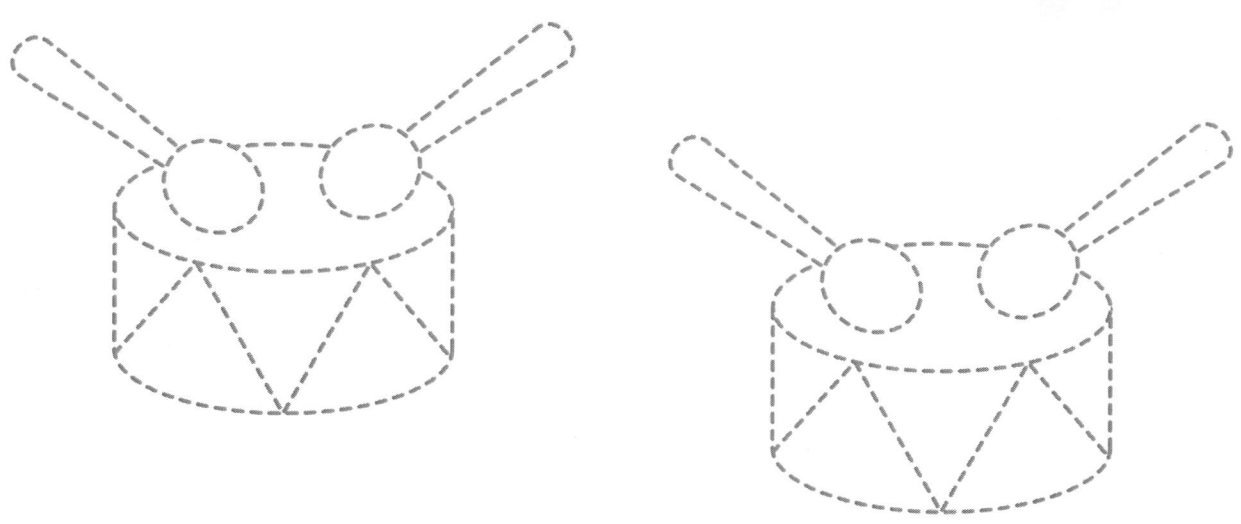

Draw

Snowman

1
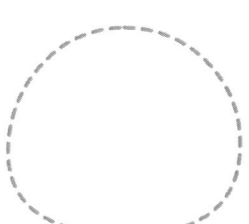

2

3

4

5

6

Trace

Draw

Airplane

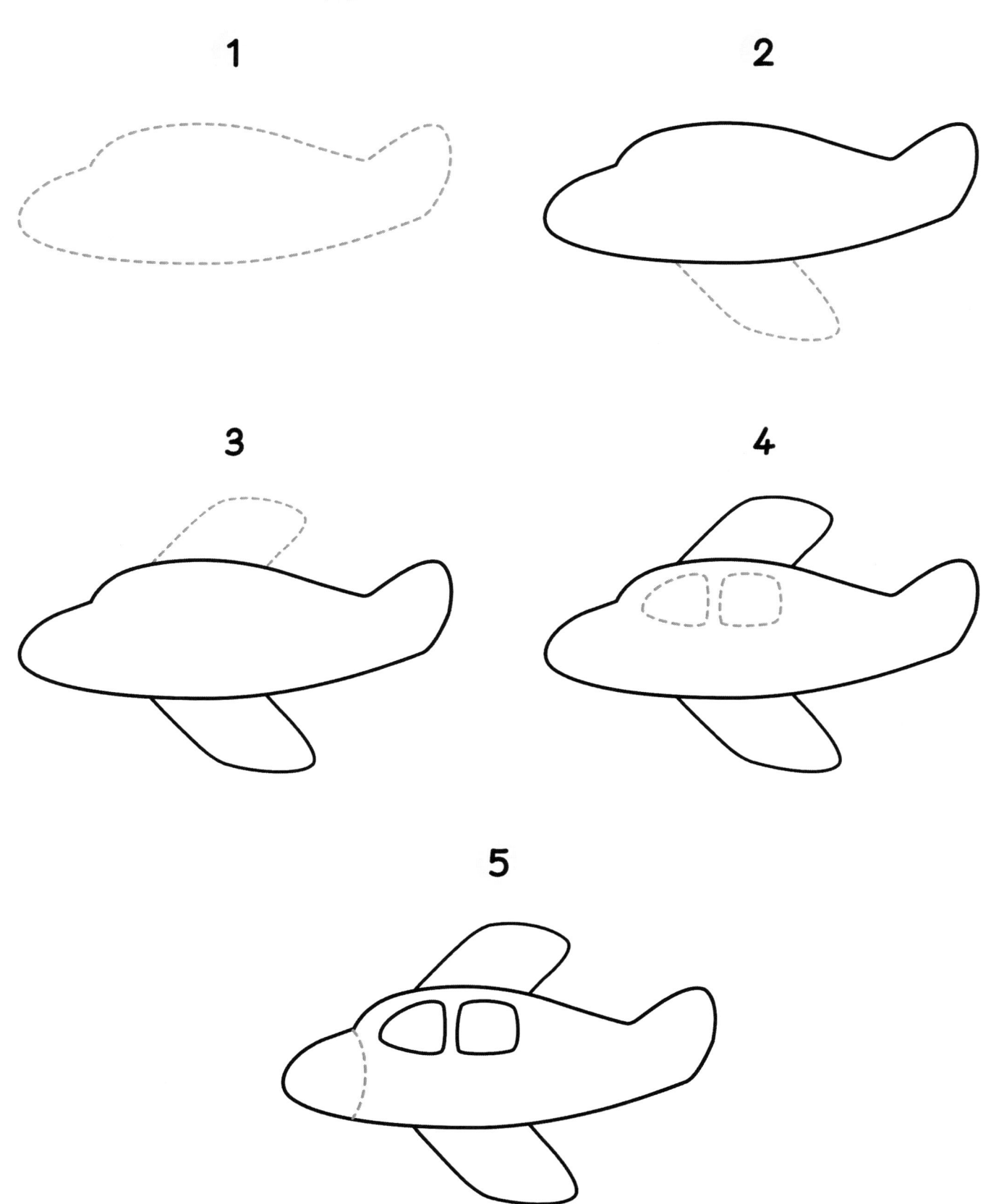

Trace

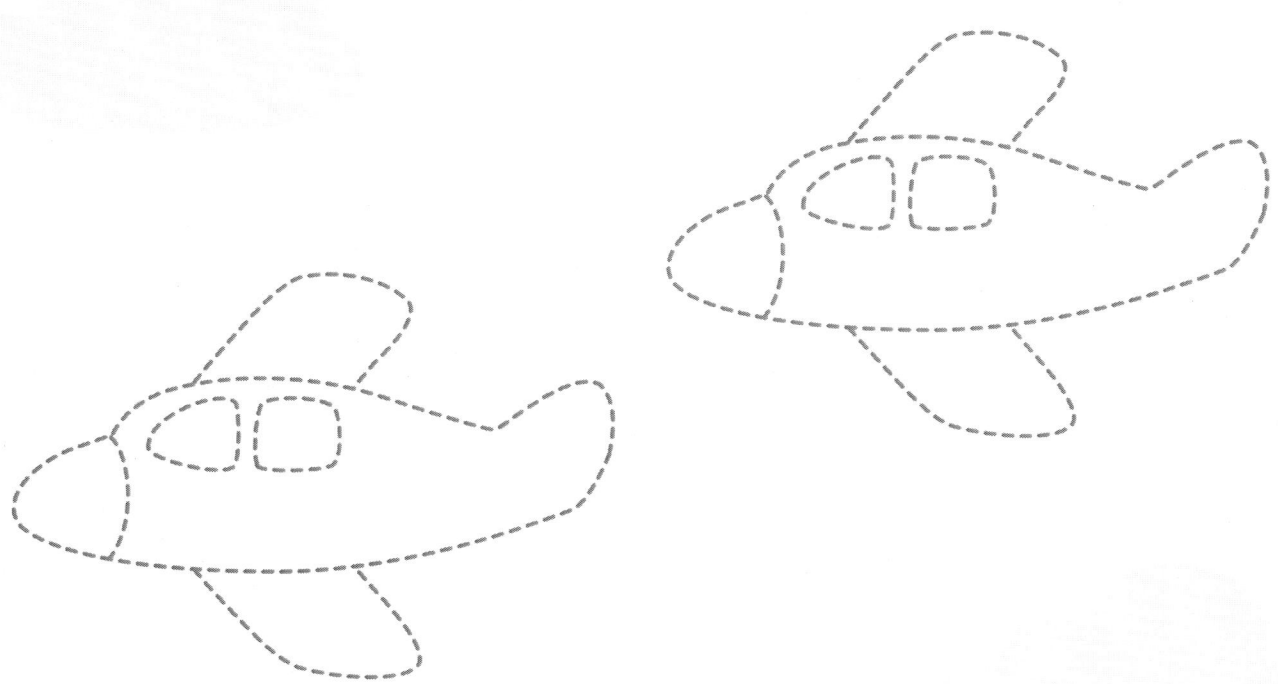

Draw

Frog

1
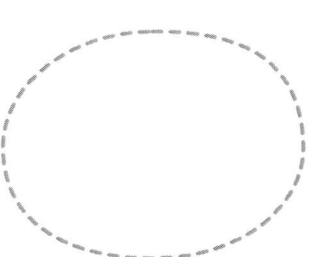

2

3

4

5

6

Trace

Draw

Turtle

1 2

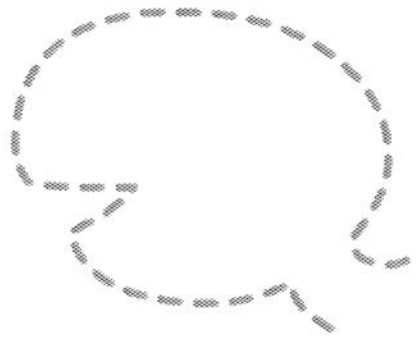

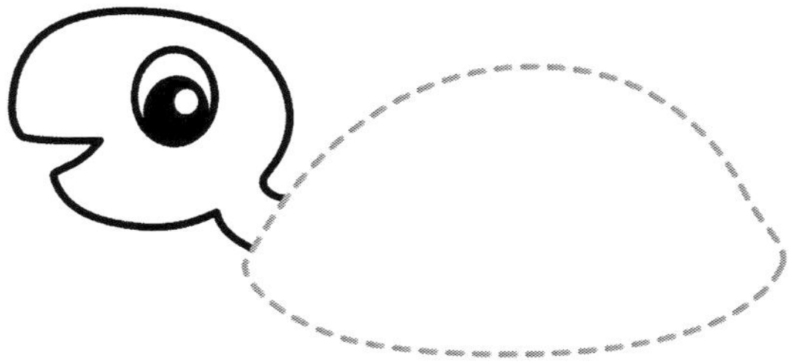

3  4

5 6

Trace

Draw

Birthday hat

1

2
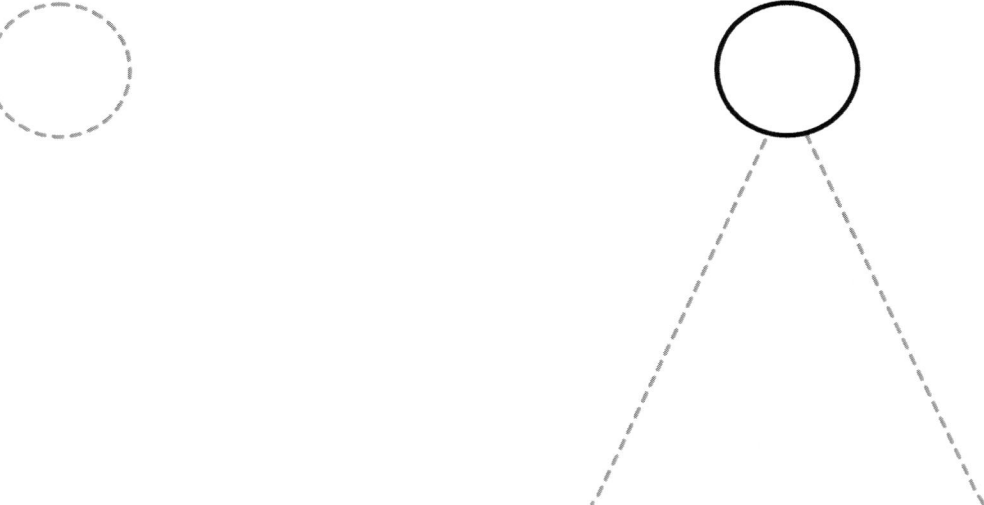

3

4
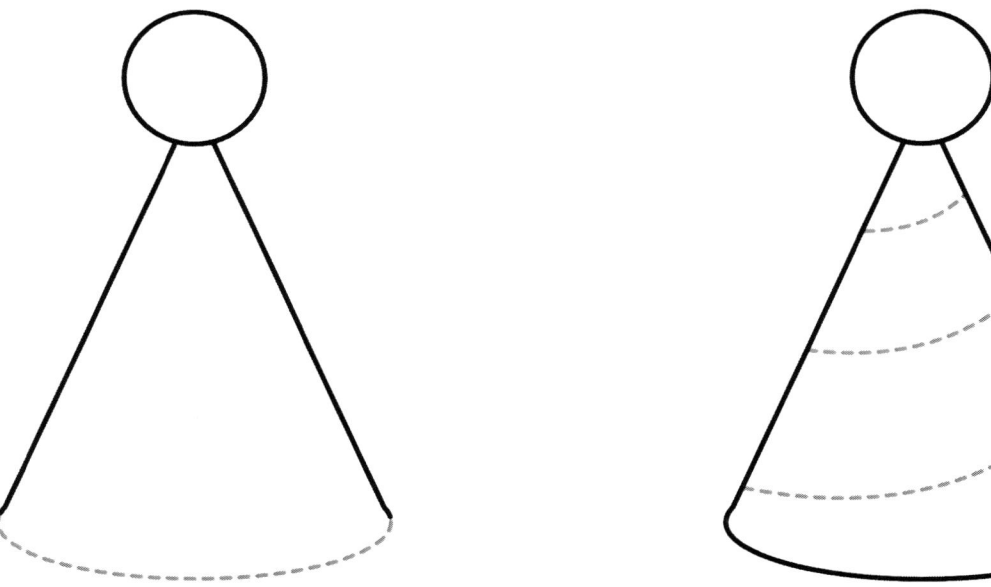

Trace

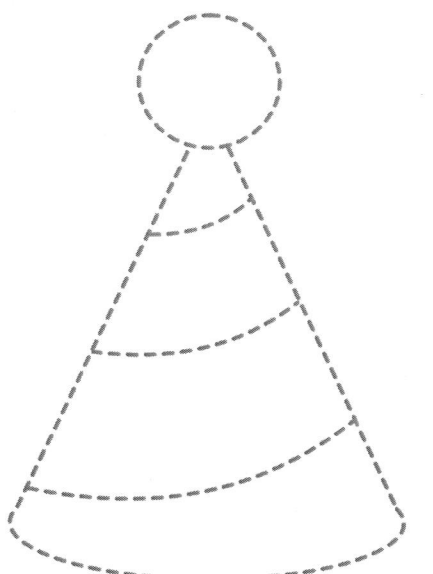 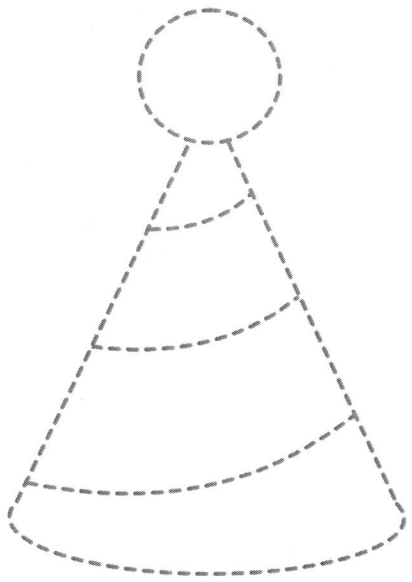

Draw

Popsicle

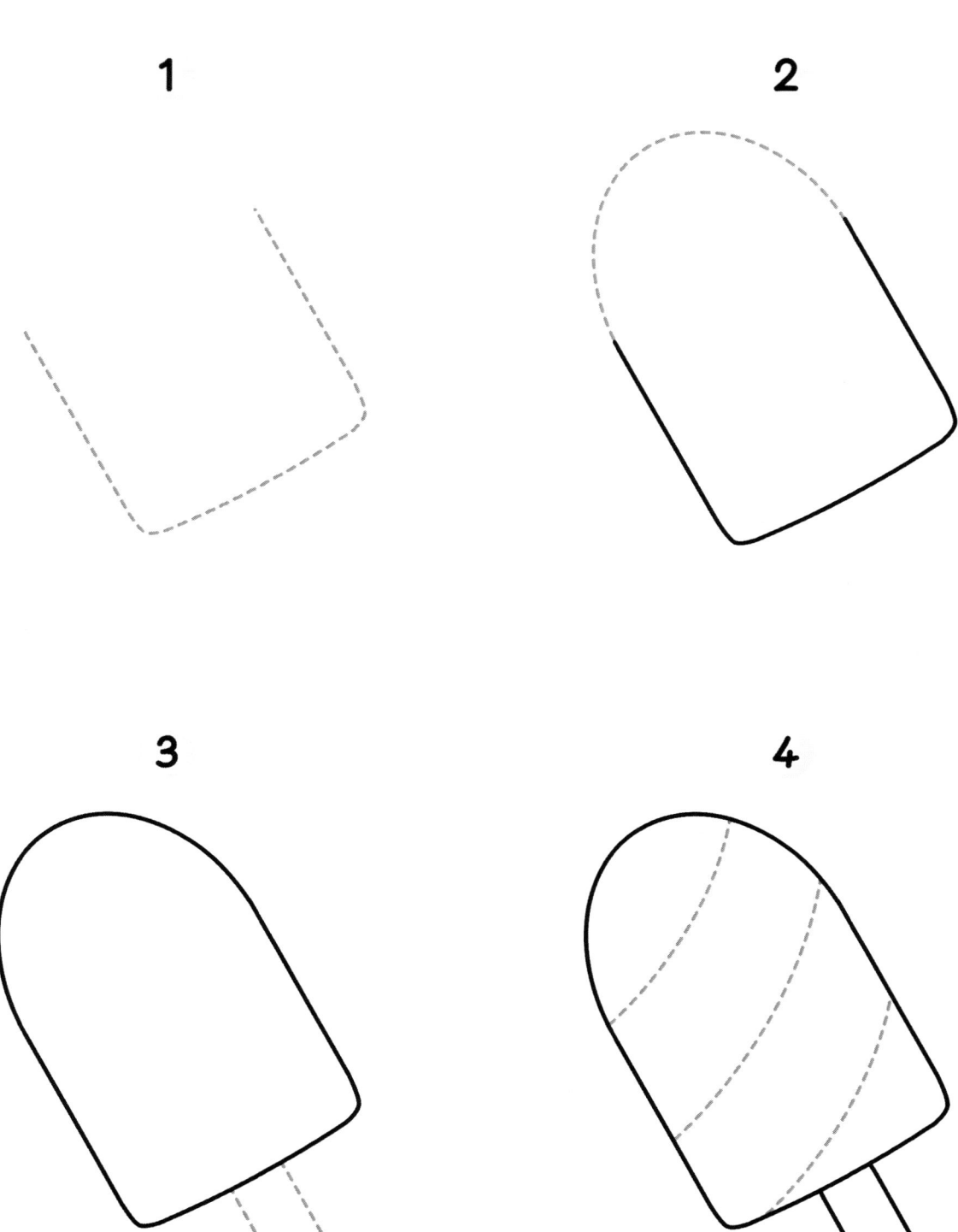

Trace

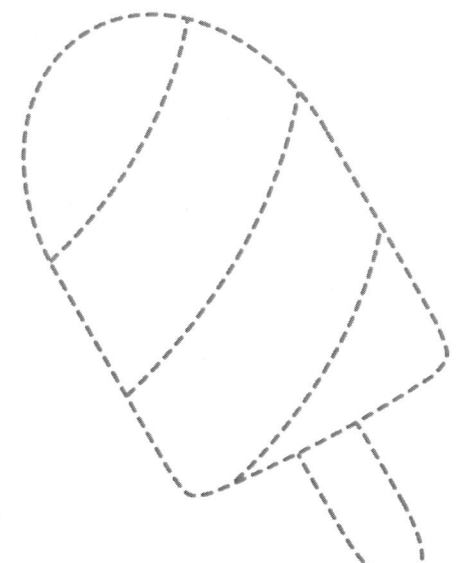 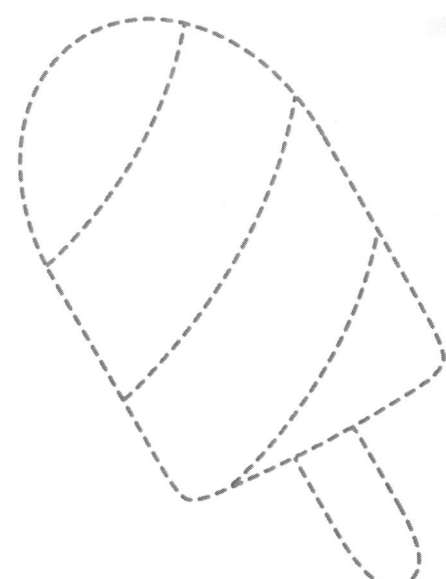

Draw

Monkey

1

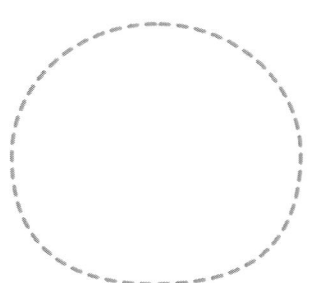

2

3

4

5

6

Trace

Draw

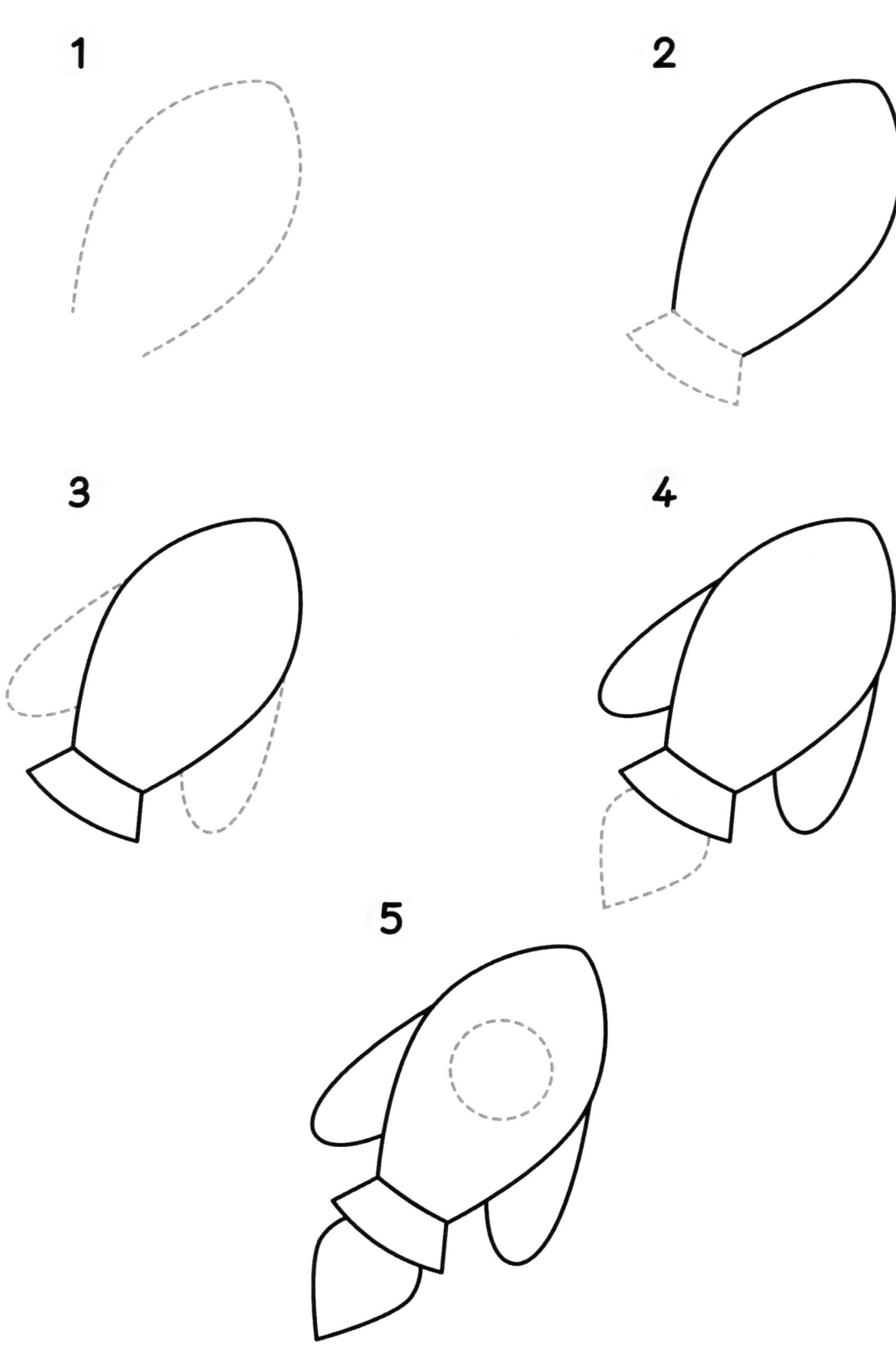

Trace

Draw

Trace

Draw

Flower

1

2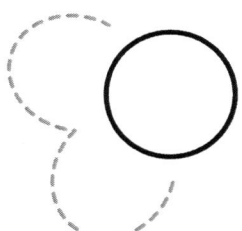

3

4

5

6

Trace

Draw

Unicorn

Trace

Draw

Car

1
2 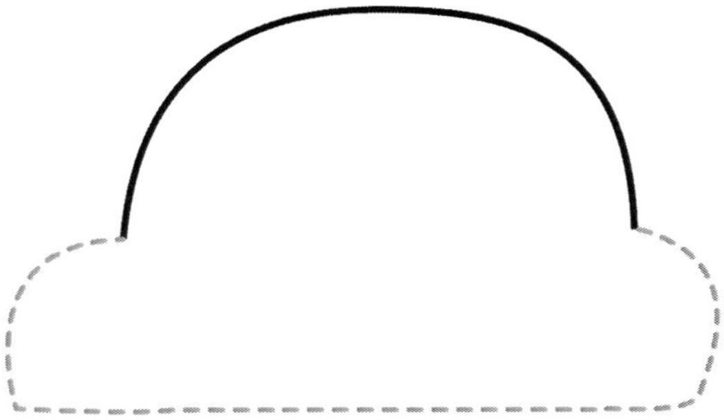
3 
4 
5

Trace

Draw

Pig

1
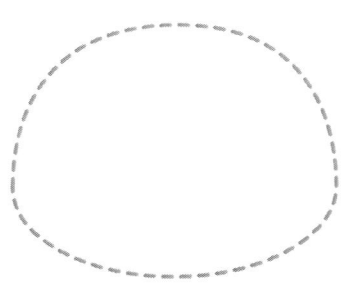

2

3

4

5

6

Trace

Draw

Sheep

1
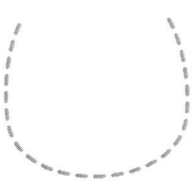

2

3

4

5

Trace

Draw

Kite

1
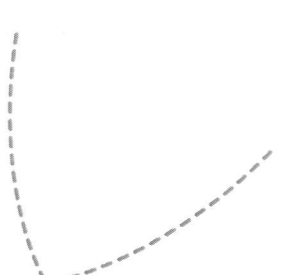

2
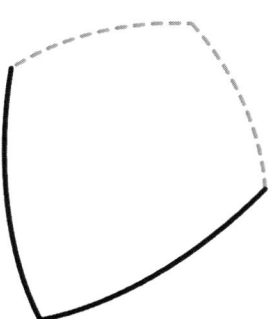

3
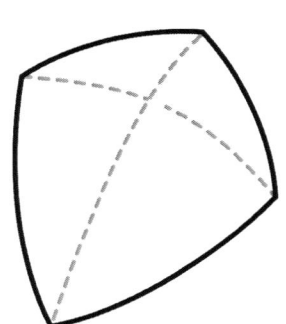

4
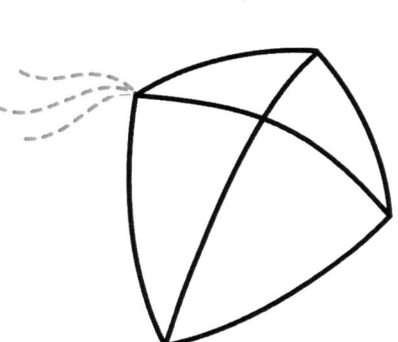

5
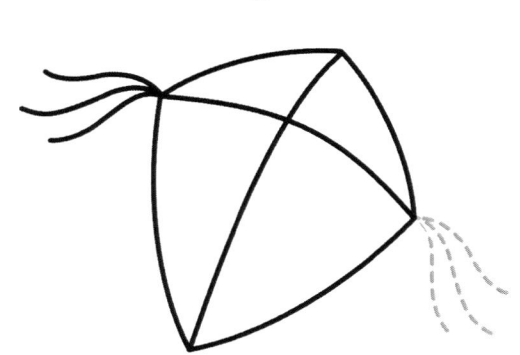

6
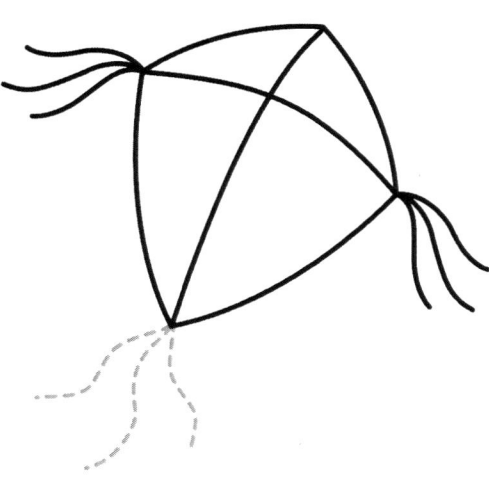

Trace

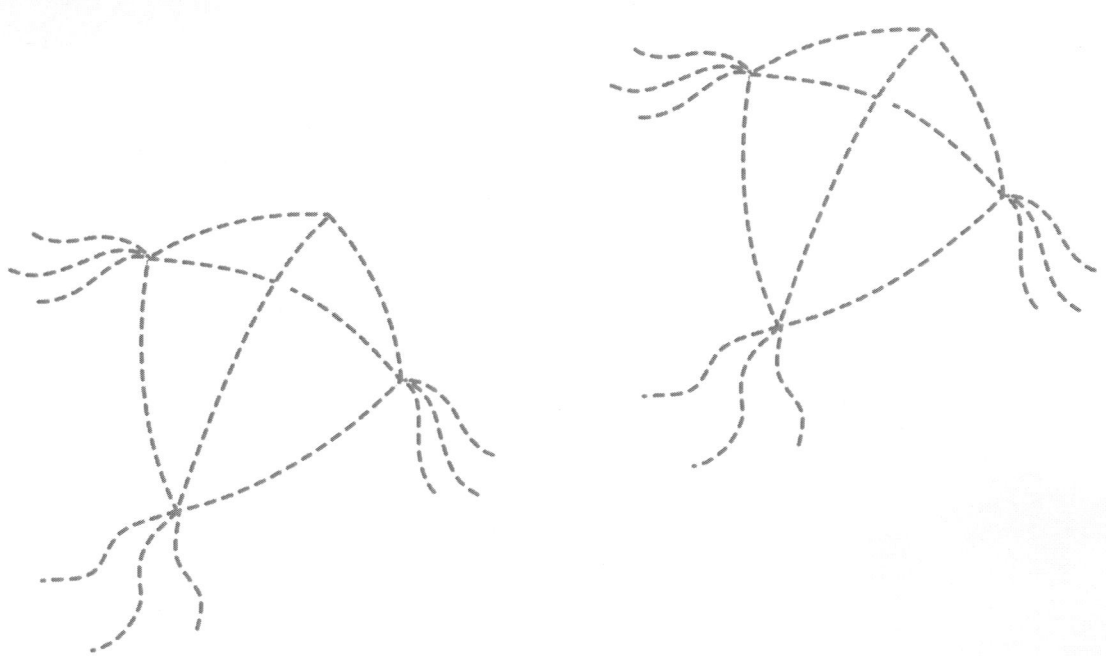

Draw

Trace and color

Dog

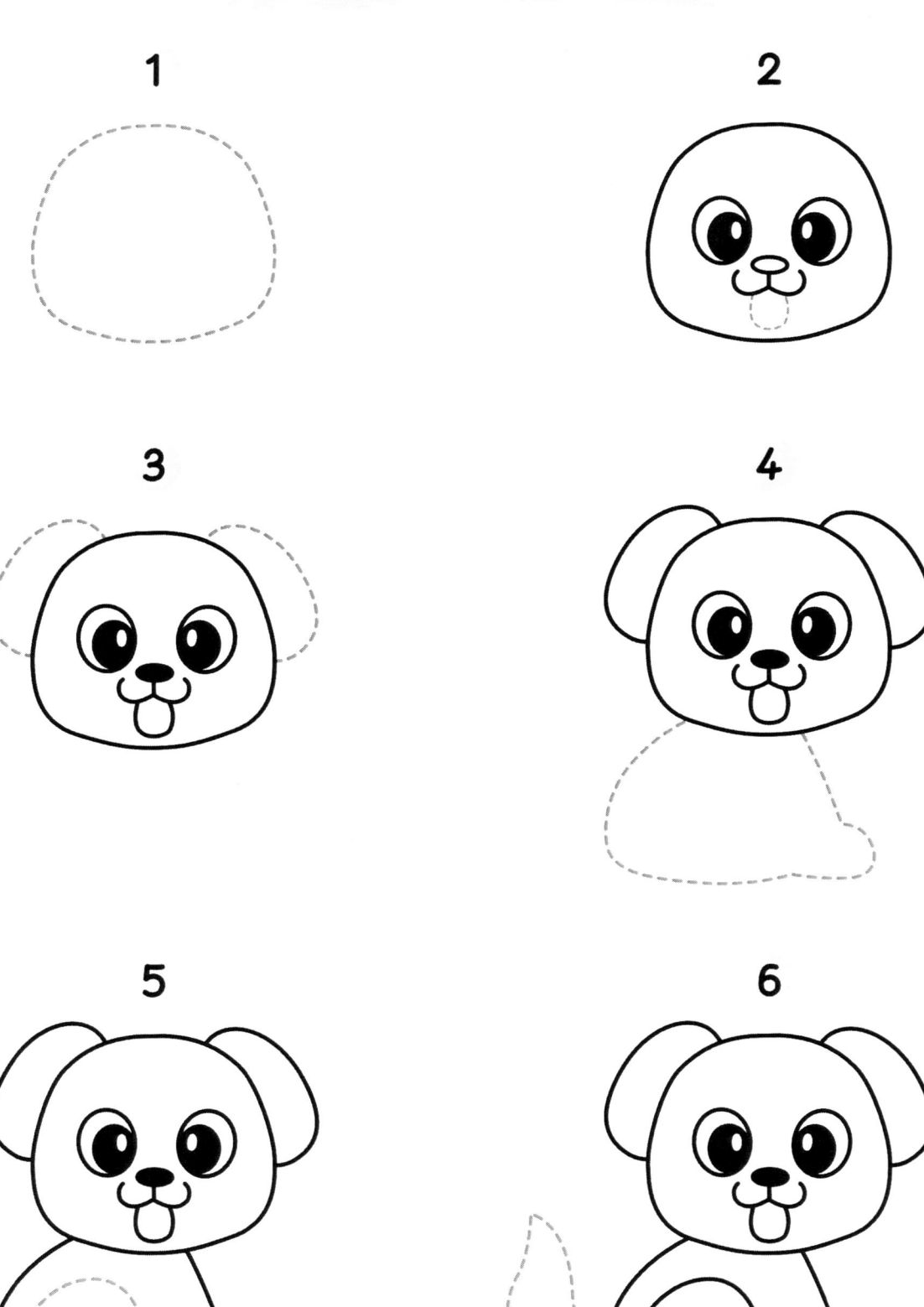

Trace

Draw

Cat

1

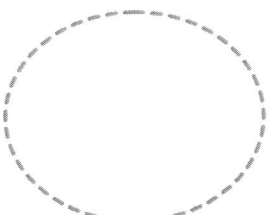

2

3

4

5

6

Trace

Draw

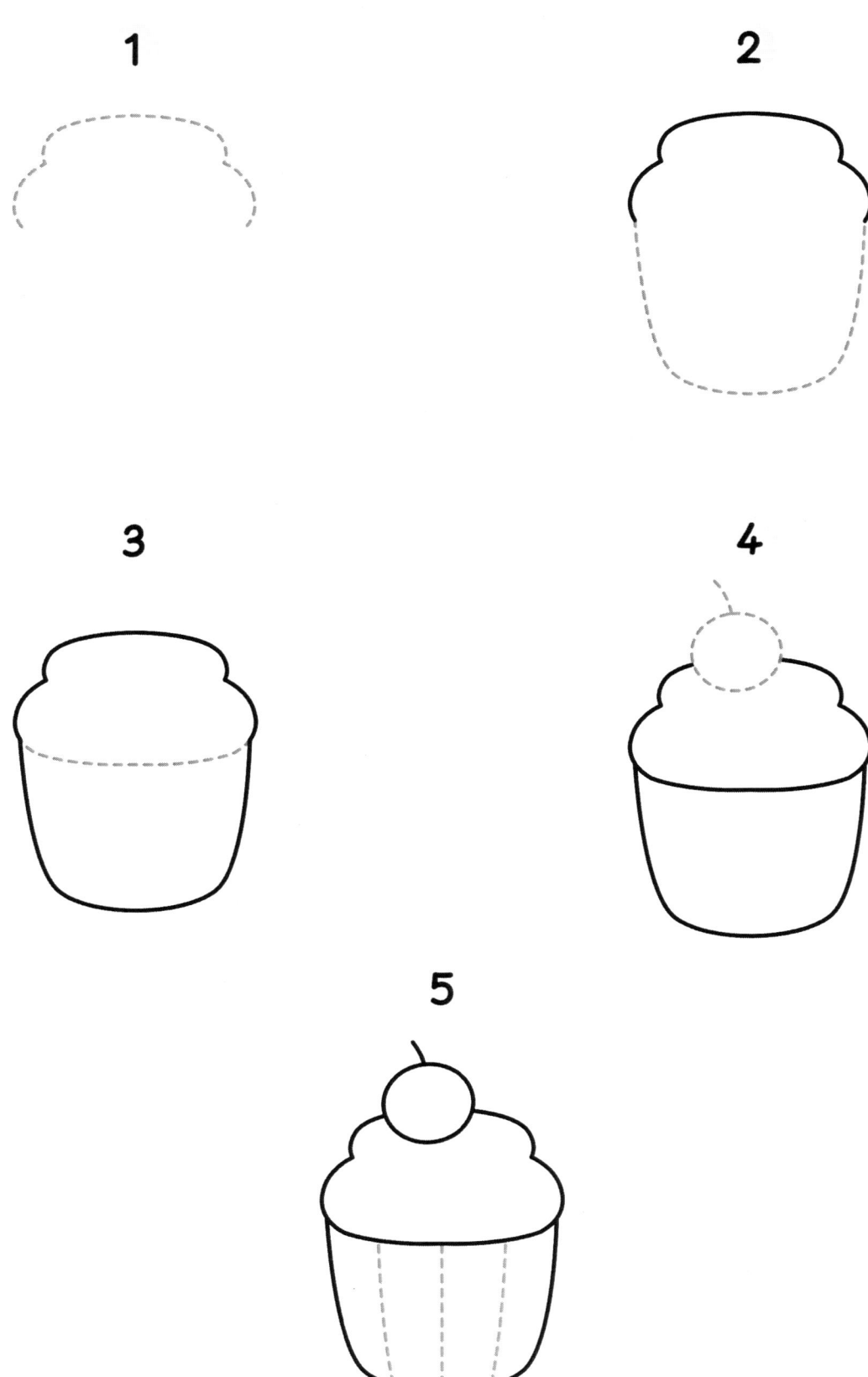

Trace

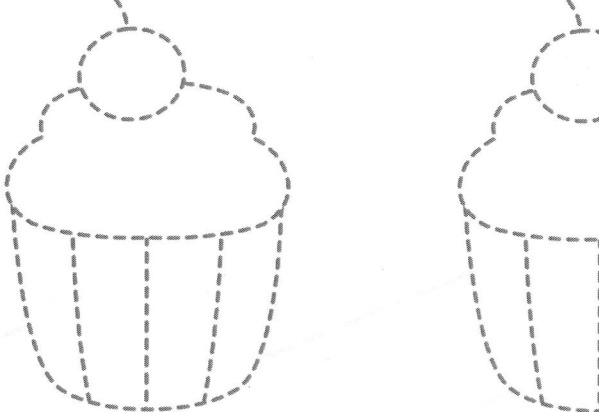

Draw

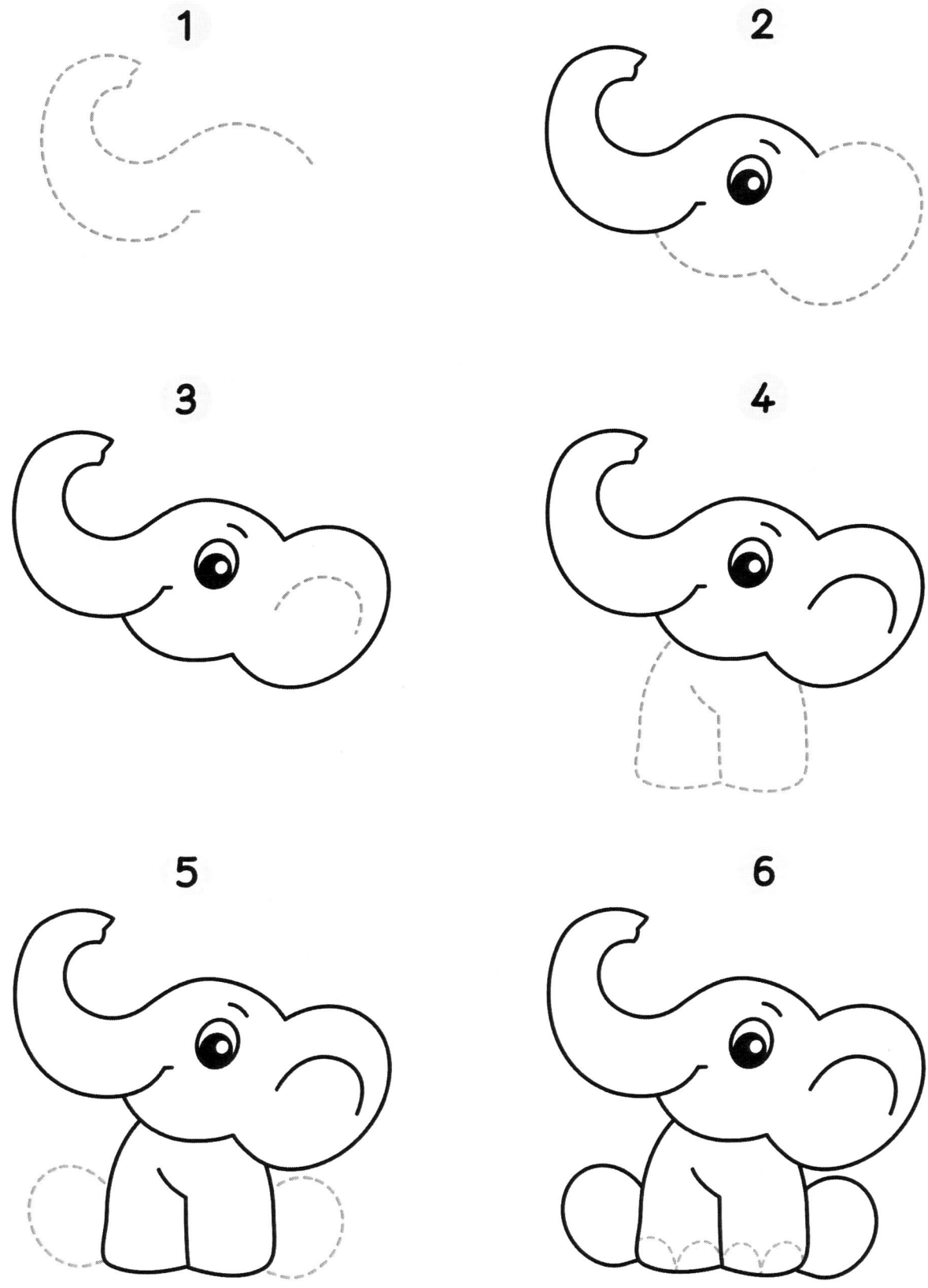

Trace

Draw

Cactus

1
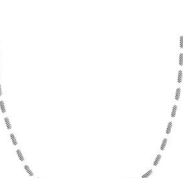

2
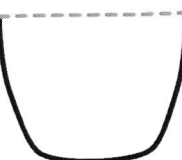

3
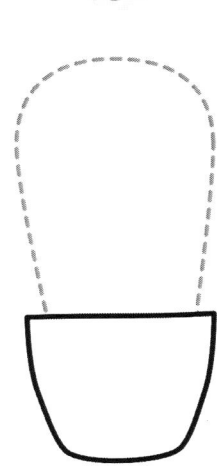

4
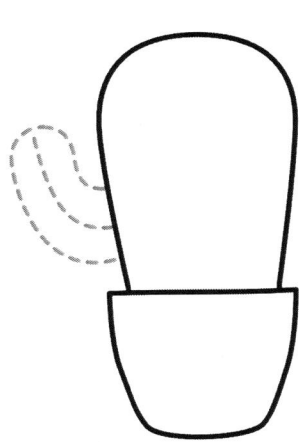

5

6
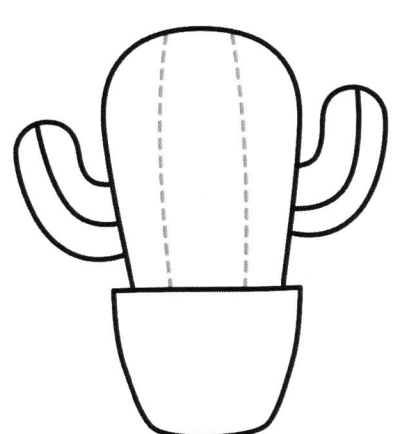

Trace

Draw

Crab

1
2
3
4
5
6

Trace

Draw

Trace

Draw

Rabbit

1

2

3

4

5

6

Trace

Draw

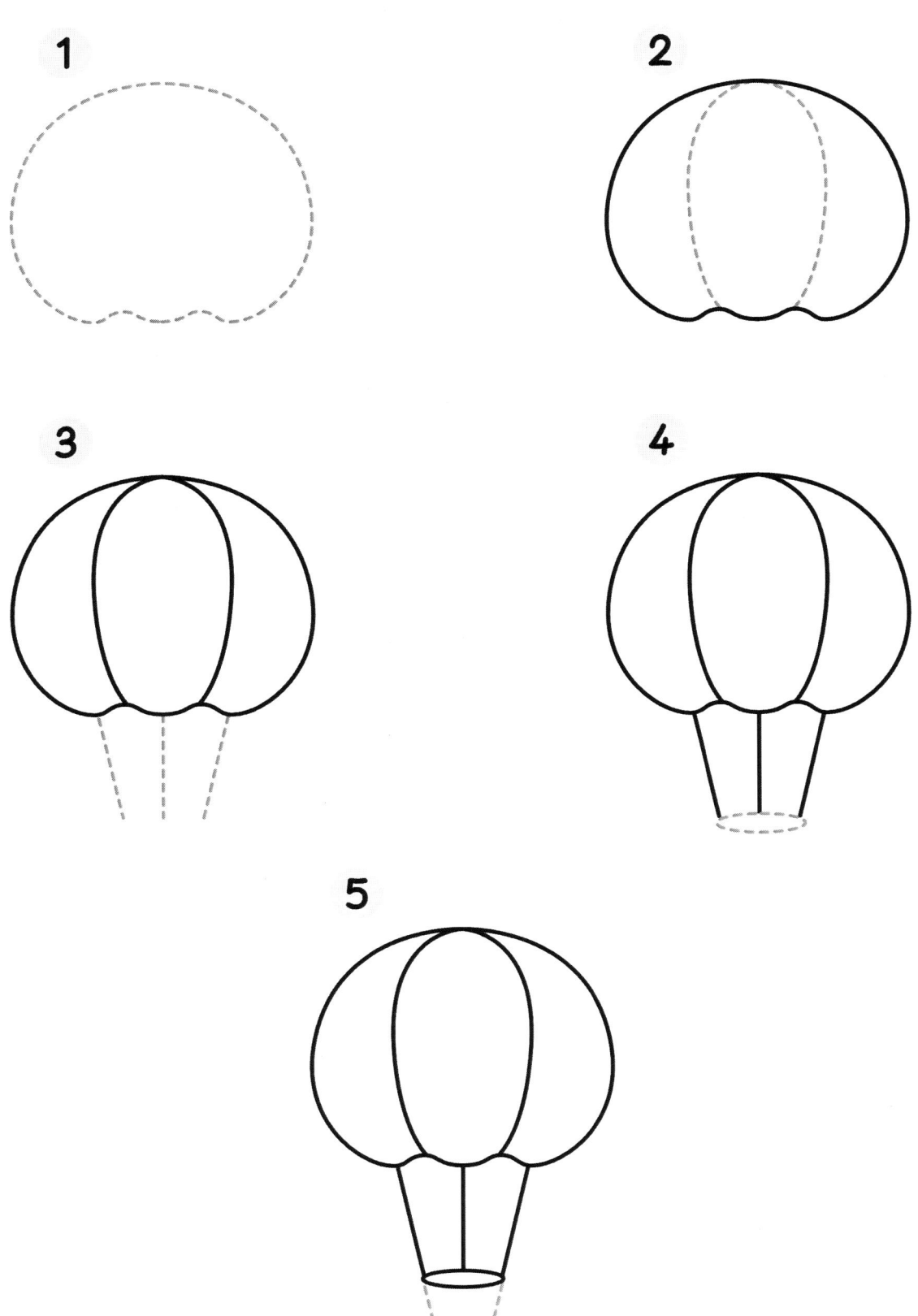

Trace

Draw

Lion

1
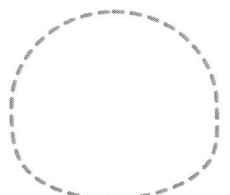

2

3

4

5

6

Trace

Draw

Tree

1
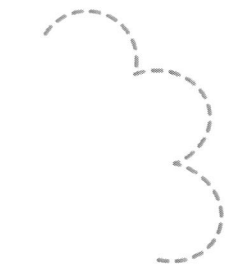

2

3

4

5

6

Trace

Draw

Hippopotamus

1
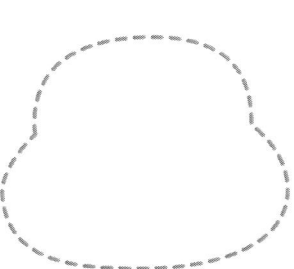

2

3

4

5

6

Trace

Draw

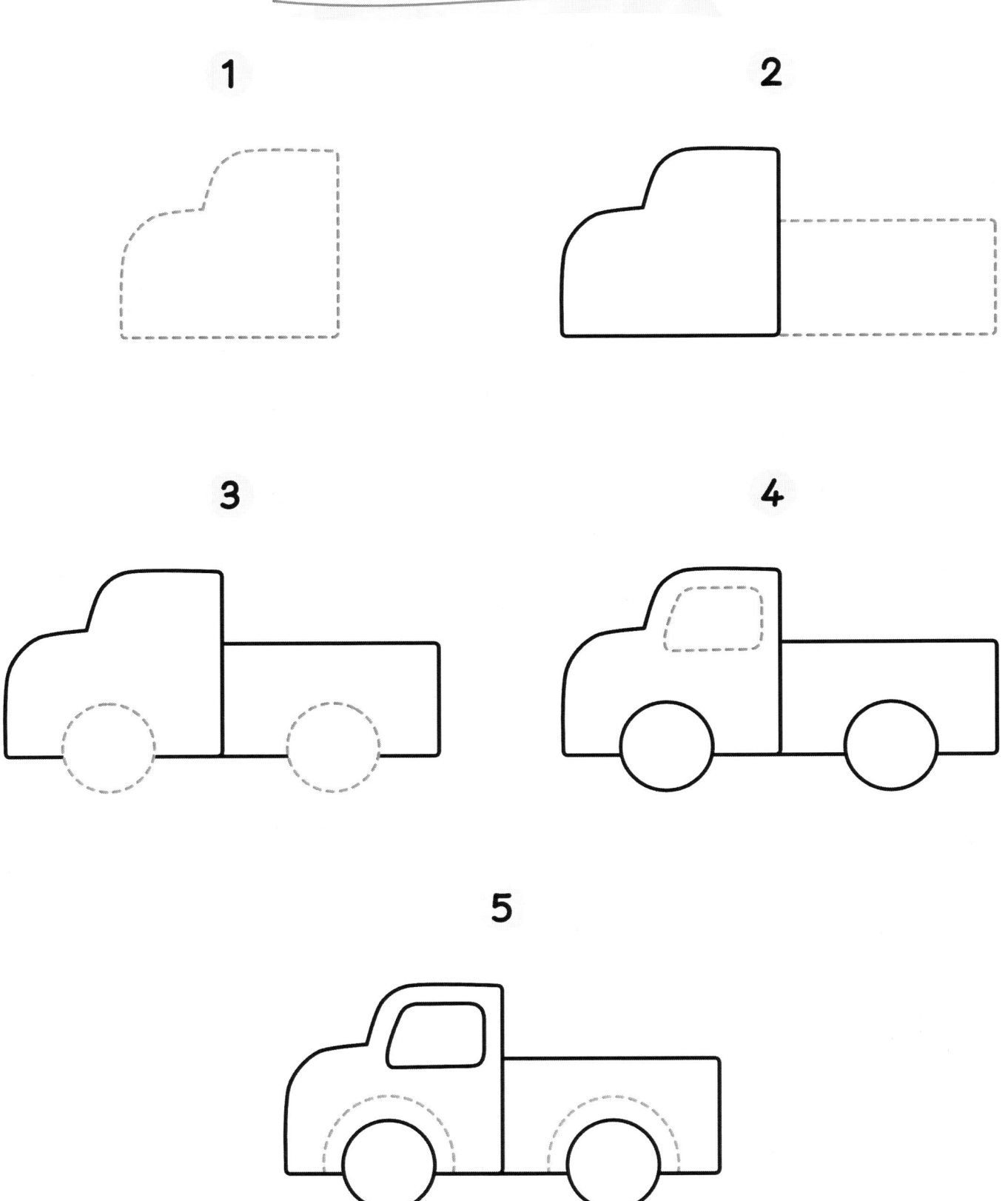

Trace

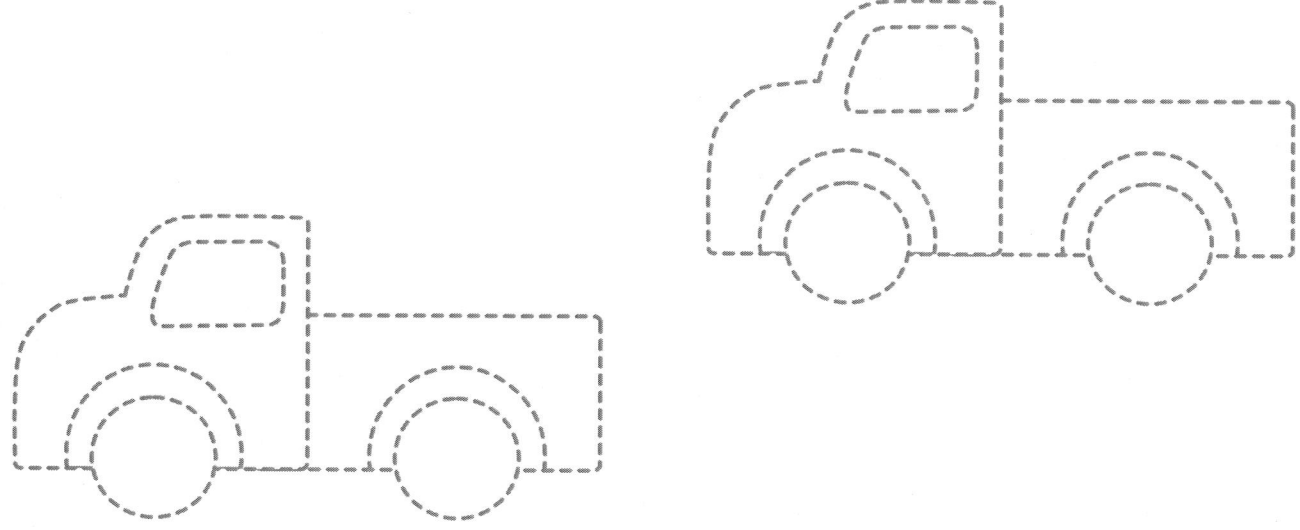

Draw

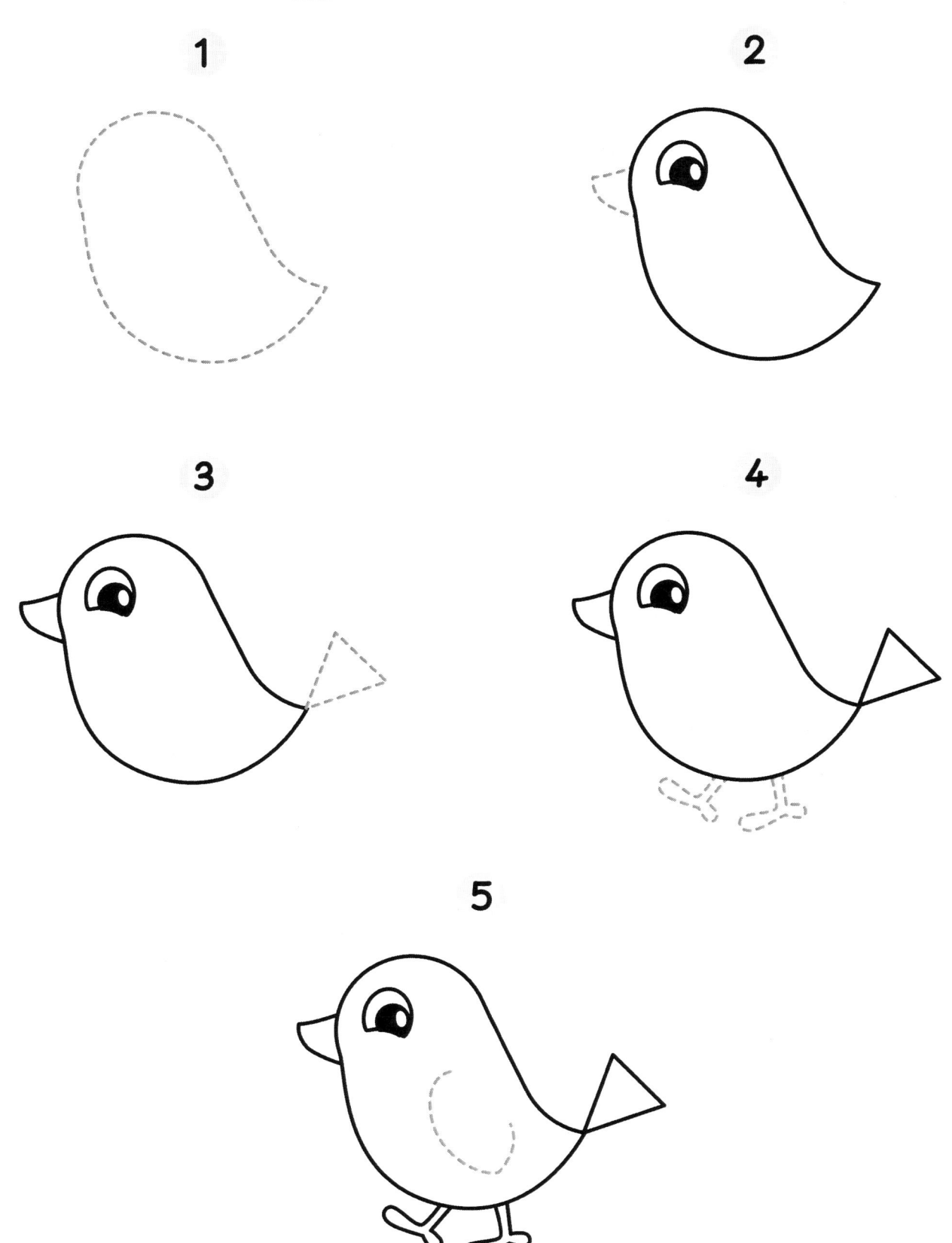

Trace

Draw

Giraffe

1

2

3

4

5

6

Trace

Draw

Cow

1

2

3

4

5

6

Trace

Draw

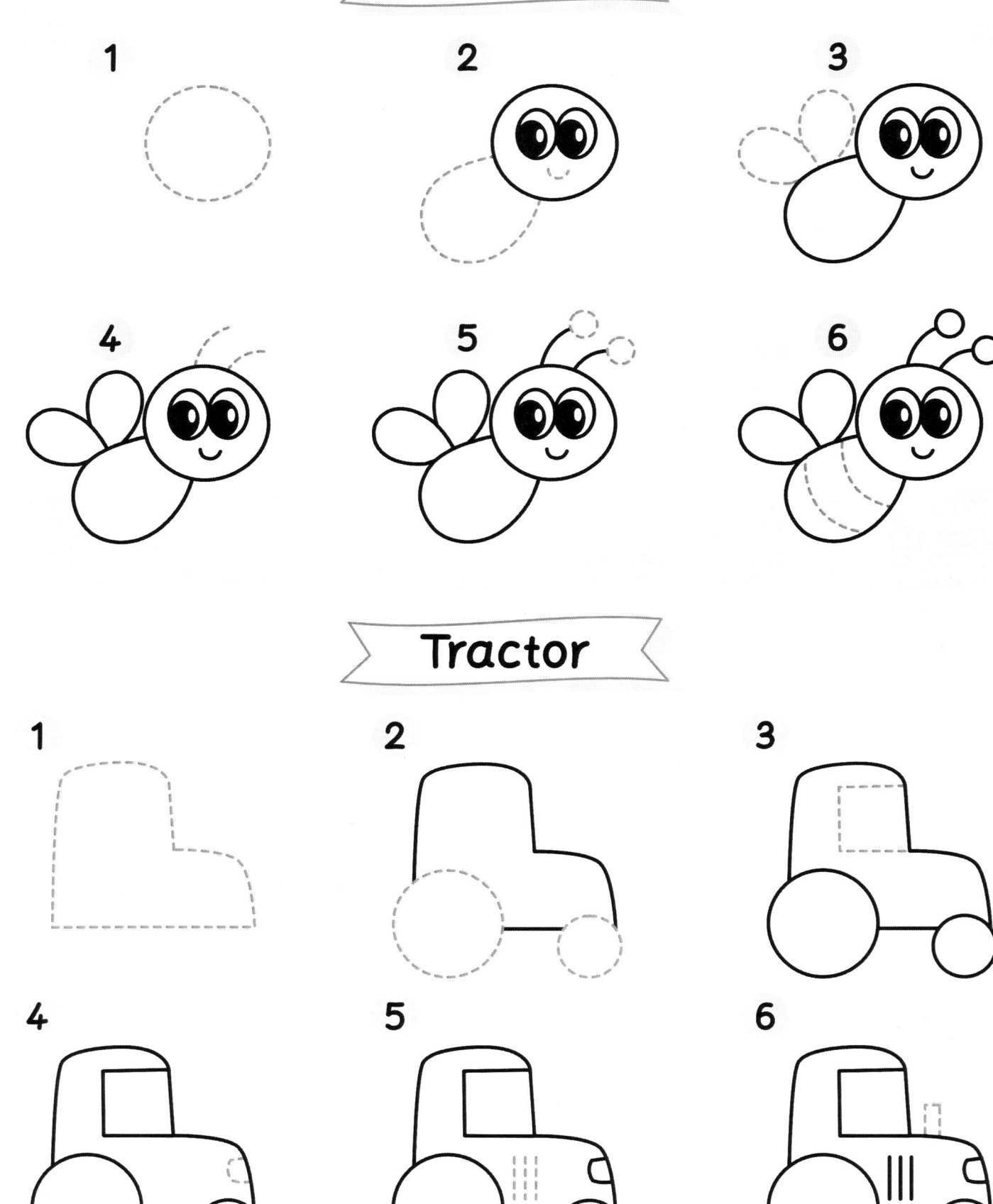

Cut from perforated lines

CERTIFICATE
OF ACHIEVEMENT

This certificate is presented to

_____

For being the master of Step By Step Drawing For Kids.

_____ _____
Date   Signature

Cut from perforated lines

Made in United States
North Haven, CT
01 November 2023

43509207R00061